BRO!!!

BRO!!!

Read More

George Criner Green

Copyright © 2020 by George Criner Green.

ISBN: Softcover   978-1-6641-4131-5
         eBook   978-1-6641-4130-8

All rights reserved. No part of this book may be reproduced or transmitted in any form or by any means, electronic or mechanical, including photocopying, recording, or by any information storage and retrieval system, without permission in writing from the copyright owner.

Any people depicted in stock imagery provided by Getty Images are models, and such images are being used for illustrative purposes only. Certain stock imagery © Getty Images.

Print information available on the last page.

Rev. date: 11/09/2020

To order additional copies of this book, contact:
Xlibris
844-714-8691
www.Xlibris.com
Orders@Xlibris.com
817465

Dedicated to my wife, "Wanda Jones Green".

Special Thanks

To the late Sergeant Froswa W. Johnson and to the artist who goes by

Contents

Introduction ix

1. Pistol Pete 1
2. White Shoes 3
3. I'm The Greatest 5
4. Another Day In The City 10
5. The Game 13
6. That Negro League 15
7. Payton (Sweetness) 17
8. The Green Lot 19
9. Winners 22
10. Dallas Cowboys 24
11. One Million Men and Me 26
12. Katy Park 29
13. Lady of the Hills 31
14. I Can 33
15. The Sun Will Rise 36
16. The Fearsome Four 38
17. Will The Thrill 40
18. That's Baseball 43
19. The Fat Lady 45
20. Ricky 48
21. The Bells of Baylor Nation 51
22. Coach 53
23. Peace 57
24. Dainian 59
25. Golden Boys 62

26. Say No 64
27. Brady 66
28. Prime Time 68
29. Jefferson Street Joe 71
30. Thoughts of Oakland 74
31. I Am Third 77
32. Juice 79

Introduction

Hello everyone, thanks for taking an interest in obtaining my third book titled

>BRO!! READ MORE.

This book was written to create an interest in men learning and having an awareness through reading. One will find within this book stories, motivational talk, inspirational messages, sport heroes and just men talk.

It's a fun book for you to enjoy. Every Man Cave needs one. Improve your thinking by reading.

Hope you enjoy it, until next time. Thank you.

Pistol Pete

He comes flying down the Court,
With wings on his feet.
The fans rise in the stands,
They yell his name, "Pete"!!!

He stops on the top of the key,
He shoots his deadly jumper.
The ball swish through the net,
No rim, he gives a fist pumper.

He runs back down the court,
Waving two fingers at the stands.
His hair looks like a mop,
He was the original showman.

He was Pistol Pete, like a gunslinger,
His jumper would shoot you dead.
It was fast as a deadly rattler,
Everyone that faced him, would dread.

He could light up the scoreboard, like no other,
No telling how many points he would score.
His movements and passes were magical,
Pete!!! Pete!!! Is what the crowd would roar.

He could outshoot Michael Jordan,
Magic and Bird could not stand in his way.
Pistol Pete was the greatest scorer in basketball,
I don't care what anyone say.

WHITE SHOES

There have been many celebrations,
By players after scoring Touchdowns.
Some would spike the ball like Homer,
Some would act like a crazy clown.

But there once was a player,
Who could put all others to shame.
He stood barely five feet nothing,
Billy White Shoes was his name.

He painted his shoes white in college,
To be different from all the rest.
He was fast like grease lighting,
He was quick and pesky as a pest.

Whenever he scored a touchdown,
He would do this little funny dance.
It looked like the funky chicken,
But it was the "White Shoes" as Billy pranced.

Do the White Shoes, Billy White Shoes,
White shoes your bad self away.
White Shoes on them Billy White Shoes,
That's what the crowd would say.

He knew how to get the crowd going,
He brought the entertainment to the game.
Everybody loved Billy White Shoes,
White Shoes, White Shoes was his name.

Billy White Shoes

I'm The Greatest

He was big, he was pretty, he was fast, he was free,
He could float like a butterfly, and sting like a bee.
His hands was fast, faster than your eyes could see.
He was the "greatest" of all the champions,
He was Mohammad Ali.

He fought Sonny Liston, who he called "the bear".
He predicted a knock out, that gave Liston a scare.
He said the bear would go down around seven.
He would knock him out, so we'll all go to heaven.

Ali knocked him out, true to his word,
He predicted a quicker knock out if a rematch occurred.
He told the world, he could plainly see,
If he fights the bear again, he'll go in three.

A rematch happened, it was over in three,
Ali knocked him out, with a punch you couldn't see.
At age 21 he became the heavyweight champ,
People from everywhere visited his camp.

He changed his name from Cassius Clay to Mohammed Ali,
Becoming a Muslim minister was what he would be.
He preached Islam, how to live and pray,
He preached about respect, being black in the world today.

They stripped him of his title, for not going to Viet Nam,
They said he wasn't a minister, they called him a scam.
Two years they barred him, but he didn't become a tramp,
He preached his message to everyone,
he became the "people's champ".

When he was reinstated, he got a match with smoking Joe,
Joe owned the title that Ali wanted so.
They fought in the big apple, at the garden
where Ali's punches joe took,
Then in round 14, Ali got caught by a mean left hook.

He went down, but he got up. The years had slowed Ali,
He lost his first fight and the crowd would all agree.
He took the loss with honor, he promised
to be the champ again,
He later fought joe twice and both times he would win.

Ali's next great fight took place in the African jungle,
He fought big George, and the two staged a rumble.
The world had seen the Ali shuffle, and the invisible punch,
But on big George, Ali would rope-a-
dope, and have him for lunch.

They fought late one night, Zaine was where they started,
When the bell rung, the love in each man parted.
Big George pounded away, and Ali would rope-a-dope,
Big George pounded for seven rounds,
for Ali, there was no hope.

By the end of round seven, Ali's plan started setting in,
The rope-a-dope was working, Big George was out of wind.
Ali hit him on the chin with a powerful right blow,
It caught Big George and sent him to the Floor.

Big George couldn't get to his feet, when the ref counted ten,
Ali won back his title and was crowned the Champ again.
He kept his title longer than anyone in the boxing game,
He beat everyone he fought that was
trying to take his fame.

Now he's retired, his life is easy and slow,
He spends time with his family,
preaching Islam and staying low.
I saw him on T.V. saying people will never learn,
"I am The Greatest There'll Ever Be,
and One Day I Shall Return!"

He was big, he was pretty, he was fast, he was free,
He could float like a butterfly, and sting like a bee.
His hands were fast, faster than your eyes could see.
He was the "greatest" of all the champions,
He was Mohammad Ali.

Ali, Ali, Ali, Ali, Ali, Ali, Ali, Ali, Ali.

Another Day In The City

Riding in the City one day, . . . *one day*
The *A's* and the Giants were about to play, ...*to play*
It was called the Battle of the Bay, ...*the Bay*
The World Series was on its way . . . *its way.*

I stopped at a store for a drink, ... *a drink*
Things started happening, made me think, . . . *me think*
All around me started to sink, ... *to sink*
Things fell on me, fast as a blink, ... *a blink.*

As I laid there on the floor, ... *the floor*
A wise old Asian stood at the door, . . . *the door*
I asked what happened, do you know, . . . *you know*
The old man said, it was a 7.4, . . . *4.*

He helped me up and said lucky man, ... *lucky man*
He was strong as he pulled my hand, . . . *my hand*
That quake was powerful, I must say, ... *must say*
The old man said, it's just another day, . . . *another day*

The power went off, all around the city, ... *the city*
Buildings were falling, it wasn't pretty, ... *wasn't pretty*
In the streets, hurt and bloody people lay, ...*people lay*
The old man said, it's just life in the bay, ... *the bay.*

An overpass had fallen on the Nimitz Freeway, ...*Freeway*
Crushing cars below like lumps of clay, ...*Like clay*
Horror fills the air around the Bay, ...*the Bay*
The old man said, life will go on everyday, ...*everyday.*

Cracks in the streets spreading the ground, ... *the ground*
People are missing can't be found, ... *be found*
Cries for help, what an awful sound, ... *awful sound*
The old man said, don't worry, help will
come around, . . . *come around.*

Candlestick is frozen, players won't play, ...*won't play*
Standing on the field they would stay, ... *would stay*
The stick might fall into the Bay, ... *the Bay,*
The old man said, life in the Bay is this way, . . . *this way.*

A cloud of darkness covered the Bay, . . . *the Bay*
There was a moment of silence to pray, ...*to pray*
The old man shook his head, his hair was gray, ...*was gray*
He quietly said, just another day in the Bay, ...*the Bay.*

He said, it's just another day, living in the Bay,
Living in the Bay things goes that way.
Life here is an adventure, happy and even gay,
It is just another day in the Bay.

The Game

You win, you loose, and you win again.
You threat both of these emotions the same.
Winning and loosing is like a coin,
It has two sides just like a game.

Heads you'll win, or, tails you'll lose,
But the coin remains the same.
Learning to accept, both of these sides,
You'll master the purpose of the game.

Your world don't end after a lost,
Just flip the coin again.
You can flip it once or flip it twice,
Just hang in there, you'll get a win.

The coin is like the game you play,
No telling what the outcome provides.
You win, you lose, so what's the big deal,
It's still a coin with two sides.

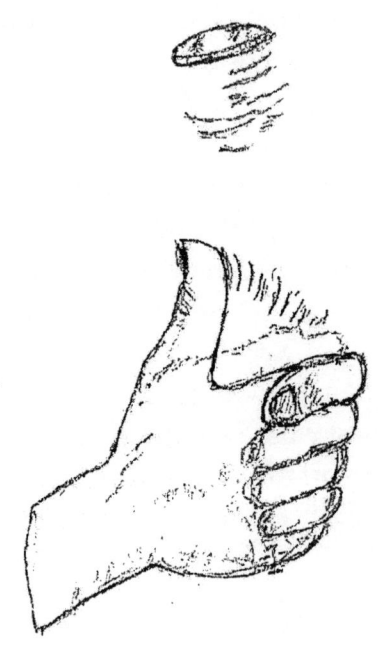

That Negro League

Who are those guys on that baseball field?
Everything they do brings cheers and thrills.
They had been playing all day, and did not get fatigued.
They are the colored players of the Negro League.

The ball passes around from hand to hand.
Very skilled players, fine tune as a band.
Full of surprises with hidden ball tricks.
You will get your money's worth, enjoying every bit.

With knickerbocker type pants, long socks and all.
Making unbelievable plays, everyone wants the ball.
High kicks from the pitchers, that reach the sky.
Like carnival magicians, they catch everyone's eye.

Everything they do, looks fun and classy.
You will get caught in the excitement as the time passes.
Playing day and night, they never get fatigued,
Those merry colored men of the Negro League.

Payton (Sweetness)

So swift, so powerful, he was beautiful to see.
He could stop on a dime, shake and bake until he was free.
He could fly over the top, the man had no weakness.
He carried that rock like no other,
they called him Sweetness.

He was built like Achilles, flawless all the way.
He would hit the line and explode,
he went hard on every play.
He was as sweet as tea, that is made in a soul food cafe.
He was as sweet as they come, that is all you could say.

He had the strength of a bull, that you would see in a rodeo.
He wasn't that fast, but quick, far from being slow.
He could cut inside and break tackles, until he's free.
One of the greatest players your eyes could ever see.

In the open field he would prance, rather than run.
He owned the football field, he was cocky as they come.
He was not that big, but he was very compact.
His uniform fitted perfectly, his shoes looked like spats.

The fans would yell "Sweetness", wherever he would go.
In response to them, he would put on a show.
His records speak for themselves, he
left everyone speechless,
Like honey on butter bread, everyone loved "Sweetness".

The Green Lot

I went to this game in Houston,
It happened on Christmas Eve.
The Texans were playing the Bengals,
With a win, the playoffs they would receive.

The Reliant was filled to capacity,
Football fans gathered everywhere.
There was a feeling of holiday spirit,
The Christmas excitement filled the air.

Fans were dressed for the occasion,
Santa, his wife and Buddy were there.
Santas helper and the grinch were snooping around,
It was fun, no one seem to care.

My trip then made a detour,
There was a commotion coming from a tent.
Inside going on was a party,
Who was in charge? I had no hint.

They had live music, food and dancing,
There was Christmas celebration all about.
Man, this group really knew how to party,
Everyone was welcome to hang out.

Later on they started dancing,
They were line dancing in the street.
People started joining in the celebration,
They were dancing and stomping their feet.

Spirits flowed like water,
They were given toasts before the game was played.
The party kept getting larger,
It was amazing how well they behaved.

One lady yelled "We are the Texans,"
In Houston Texas this is how we roll.
Someone yelled "You tell them sister,"
Here in the Green lot we got control.

True, they were wild, but controllable,
I felt welcome just sitting down.
These guys really know how to tailgate,
That is how they roll in that Houston town.

Winners

A Winner is a person,
Who does not brag or complain.
One that works the hardest,
And takes pride in playing the game.

A Winner lifts the spirits,
Of everyone on the team.
One who has the courage and the faith
That makes a coach's dream.

A Winner never loses,
He looks forward for the next day.
A Winner never argues or cries,
A Winner makes the big play.

A Winner believes in himself
And trusts God to carry him on.
A Winner is a leader, a hero,
A Winner is a champion.

Dallas Cowboys

(Victory Parade)

When "Da Boys" come home for the Bowl,
The streets will shine like gold.
Confetti will fall, the President will call,
When "Da Boys" come home from the Bowl.

When the parade goes down the street,
"Da Boys" will ride four deep.
Bands will be jamming, the streets will be cramming,
As the crowd cheers on their feet.

This day, Big "D" will stand still,
Seeing the boys, what a thrill.
The fans will stand for the fairest in the land,
"Da Boys" are King of the Hill.

Fans from miles will be there,
What the weather may be, no one cares.
Kids will miss school, they will say it's cool.
There will be speeches from the Mayor.

Everyone will wear Silver and Blue,
Their love for "Da Boys" runs true.
Young folks and old will hear the stories retold,
How "Da Boys" victory came through.

Oh what a day it will be,
Seeing "Da Boys", the Fans, and Me.
Call the Police for extra patrols,
When "Da Boys" come from the Bowl.

One Million Men and Me

Early one Monday Morning,
I heard the sound of marching feet.
So loud, so powerful, and so mighty,
The sound moved with a magical beat.

As I looked out my door all puzzled,
There was a sight so beholding to me.
As far as I could see, there was blackness,
One Million Men came marching toward me.
Marching and marching toward me.
As far as I could see,
They came marching and marching toward me.

They showed pride, joy and laughter,
A million brothers with ideas and goals.
I saw gang bangers marching arm and arm,
There was the rich, homeless and old.

From miles and miles, they kept coming.
They marched east, toward Washington D.C.
They talked about atonement and unity,
As One Million Men, marched passed me.
Yes, they marched, right pass me.
Marching and marching pass me,
As far as I could see,
They came marching and marching pass me.

They said, today is a day of recollection,
Who we are, what we are, and getting there.

We have to remember, we're Brothers,
If we don't help each other, who's going to care?

We pledge to be non-violent and self improved.
No more black on black offense.
We pledge to take care of our sisters.
To me, what they said made sense.

As they passed, I felt so welcome,
I'd never seen anything like it before.
There was no shooting, fighting, or profanity,
I'd joined in with the march to hear more.

There I was, surrounded by my Brothers.
I was feeling Black, Proud and Free. We
stood One Million Strong at the capitol.
That's *One Million Men and Me.*
Yes, *One Million Men and Me*,
Marching and Marching with me.
As far as I could see,
One Million Men Marching-Plus Me.

Katy Park

O Katy how I remember,
Your warm summer nights.
How the late train would hold up traffic,
How the birds played tag in your lights.

The smell of popcorn and hot dogs,
The sound of vendors selling pops and cold beer.
The hustle of ball boys running after foul balls,
The laughter of the Crowd and Cheer.

You were the home of the Red Legs and Pirates,
You had visitors called Texans and All Stars.
There were stories of you housing Satchel and Jackie,
I remember stories of Jessie Owen out running cars.

That Green Monster that surrounded you,
It was a challenge for every hitter to see.
The thrill of knocking a ball onto Webster or 8th Street,
The excitement of hearing the Ump-yell-strike Three!

Every kid had dreams of playing on you,
But time vanish dreams away.
I will always remember the joy you brought, Dear Katy,
In my heart you will always stay.

Lady of the Hills

There's a legend of old, about the Hills in Cameron Park,
Of a beautiful lady, that walks the hills around dark.
Where she comes from, no one has any idea,
She walks alone at night, through the hills without fear.

She's tall and slim, with hair black as the night,
It touches her shoulders and glows in the moonlight.
Her skin is golden brown, smooth and tan,
She walks like a Goddess over-seeing her land.

She never speaks, she only smiles when she passes,
She flows with the wind, through trails of dried grasses.
So graceful, so lovely, so completely in control,
Only at night will she take her evening stroll.

My lady so fair, please give me thrill,
Of walking with you, through these dark lonely hills.
Tell me your secret that's hidden within,
Are you a spirit, an illusion, a hoax, or a friend?

She chooses not to speak, she only glances my way,
Just to hear the sound of her voice,
wondering what she'll say,
She kept walking and walking in her usual direction,
I watched her disappear in the moonlight reflection.

She vanished like she appeared, from nowhere it seems.
Ghost like, she disappeared like a character in a dream.
The story of her legacy may never be fulfilled,
This strange and lovely lady of the Cameron Park Hills.

I Can

I can climb a Mountain,
To it's highest peak.
I can sail the Seven Seas
That the sailors seek.

I can swim the Oceans,
A lake, river, or pond.
I can run the extra mile,
I can finish a marathon.

I can fly with the eagles,
Well, in a plane I can.
I can out think the slyest fox
Ever known to man.

I can be a leader,
I can lead others right.
I can stand and defend myself
When it's time to fight.

I can be a follower,
A small member on the team.
I can give all I've got
To help achieve it's dream.

I can carry the burdens,
The burdens of life each day.
I can go through, over, or around,
Anything in my way.

I can write, sweet music,
Play an instrument or sing a song.
I can bring a message,
And my message won't be long.

I can help the lives,
Of people who are in need.
I can give my time and talent
For the mouths to feed.

I can create miracles,
If God wants me to.
I am thankful for everything,
Especially the things I can do.

The Sun Will Rise

The game was long, everything went wrong,
It was a day of rejection and sorrow,
Good luck you've missed, but I'll guarantee you this,
The sun will rise tomorrow.

The game you lost, it came with a cost,
There's no need for pain or sorrow.
Tomorrow brings new light, you can start a new fight,
Because the sun will rise tomorrow.

The sun comes and goes, across the heavens it flows,
It's bright and there no need for mourning.
It always rise at dawn, full of life and fun,
The sun will be there each morning.

It's a symbol of goodwill, merry hearts it fills,
It rolls and play the day away.
It may hide behind a cloud but it stands high and proud,
It rules the heavens all day.

When the evening comes, it's work is done,
To have light, you'll have to borrow.
There's nothing like sunlight to make your spirits bright,
Cause the sun will rise tomorrow.

THE FEARSOME FOUR

They were four defensive linemen,
That played on the west coast shore.
They played a brand of football,
That no one had seen before.

They were four large mighty warriors.
A band of brothers searching for a war.
They were nightmares for their opponents,
Because opponents couldn't move the ball very far.

Every play they would meet at the quarterback.
When they sacked him, they would keep a score.
No team on earth could contain them,
They were known as the Fearsome Four.

The game was their church each Sunday.
Two were preachers, one a deacon and one ushers the door.
They brought fear into the game of football,
They were fearless, the Fearsome Four.

A bust was made of each of them,
That rest in the hall of fame.
Their ghosts walk around at night,
Bullying others into playing a game.

They revolutionize defensive linemen play.
They just wouldn't let other teams score.
They were the badest men to play on turf,
They were the Fearsome Four.

Will The Thrill

Hitting a ball with a bat
To some is hard to do.
If you try it yourself
You will probably find it is true.

But there was a man that played the game,
Who turned hitting in to an art.
He had the prettiest swing from the left side,
He was "Will the Thrill Clark"

He was a true natural playing baseball,
He could field, catch and do it all.
He could hit frozen ropes off every pitch,
"Will the Thrill" always answer the call.

His swing was pure as honey.
To him hitting was a piece of cake.
Some say he was the best of all times,
Pitchers dread seeing him at the plate.

Will intimidated all opposing pitchers,
With his rituals entering the batter's box.
With his foot he would draw a line in the dirt,
He wore those old school baseball socks.

He would pull his right sleeve towards his shoulders,
He held his bat high over his head.
With his right foot pointed toward the plate
He waited patiently for a dead red.

He would watch the pitcher wind-up,
Releasing a rocket inside and low.
Will would stand there eyeing that rock,
He would then let that sweet swing go.

Like the sound of a loud explosions,
As his bat connected with the ball.
The ball looked like a cruise missile,
Bouncing off the outfield wall.

Will could hustle the bases with the best of them,
He always slid hard into the base.
He would dust himself off and tip his hat,
He kept a big smile on his face.

Some where down there in the deep, deep South,
There is a man standing tall.
He is the owner of a big silver bat,
He won destroying baseballs.

There once was a fat man that sung the blues,
That enjoyed a place called Blueberry Hill.
Blueberries may be sweet but they can't compete,
With that sweet swing of Will The Thrill.

Will The Thrill

That's Baseball

Keep your head down, wait for the big hop,
Keep your eyes on the ball.
Now grab that grounder and throw to the base,
That's how you play Baseball.

Step to the plate, dig yourself in,
Take a pitch and listen for the umps call.
It may be a ball or may be a strike,
Don't panic it's just baseball.

The squeeze play is on, the blunt is down,
You try to make a play but you fall.
Hustle back up and keep you head,
It's nothing, it's just baseball.

It's the bottom of the ninth, you at bat,
A hit will win the game and all.
But you strike out and fail, O well,
Hang in there, it's just baseball.

You are pitching a great game into the late innings,
You are tired and can hardly throw the ball.
Suck it up bro, your best stuff just throw,
That's the way you play baseball.

When the game is over, relax and exhale,
Treat winning and losing the same.
Don't dwell on results, there will be another day,
That's baseball, man what a game.

THE FAT LADY

A big dark cloud rested over the stadium that day,
The boys were losing with little time to play.
As cold wet wind blew snow all around,
Viking horns were blowing, creating a haunting sound.

In the huddle, things were quiet, still and scary,
Then Rodger looked at Drew and said "Hail Mary!!"
They broke with a clap and went to the line,
The clock was running, they were short on time.

Rodger took the snap and threw a rocket to the sun,
The ball looked like a bullet shot straight out of a gun.
Far down the field it flew on its trip,
When Nat the cornerback slipped, and
drew caught it on his hip.

Drew ran into the end zone holding on to the ball.
It was a touchdown, the referee made the call.
Time ran out, the boys won the game,
That's when a large lady stood up and started to sing.

She was graceful as a peacock when it spreads its feathers.
Her voice was lovely, like a bird in the meadows.
There was a pride about her, she had everyone's love.
The crowd remained quiet hearing her song from above.

When she finished singing, people started going home,
The game was over, it ended with her song.
I said to myself, this is a very strange thing,
That was the day, I heard the Fat lady sing.

Sing your song Big Mama, sing your song.
Let them know it's over, it's time to go home.
To the victors it's lovely, to the losers it went wrong,
You can turn out the lights, when she sings her song.

Ricky

There have been many thieves in the game of baseball,
Who took pride in themselves, stealing bases and all.
There was Kirk Flood, Murry Wills, just to name a few,
Ty Cobb, Papa Bell, all their respect is due.

Many stories of base stealing are told overtime.
They stole bases for fun, it wasn't a crime.
Then alone came a player, who put them all to shame.
He was king of the base path, Ricky
Henderson was his name.

Ricky was cool, he carried himself with grace.
His uniform fitted perfect, everything always in place.
From his head to his foot, there was greatness all about.
The diamond was his kingdom,
pitchers had Better watch out.

He was a lead off hitter, who would get on base.
He would take a lead off 1st, setting the pace.
With a wide open stance, he eyed the pitcher and ball.
You knew what was coming next, the
ump was ready to make the call.

With cat like quickness, Ricky was running to 2nd base.
He slid head first, as fans went crazy in the place.
He stood straight up and waved to the stands.
Wherever he played, Ricky had many fans.

He could steal 2nd, 3rd and even home plate,
He stole so many bases, his records stand to this date.
Put all the thieves together, throw in
Alexander Monday for fun,
They all were chumps, compared to Ricky Henderson.

The Bells of Baylor Nation

The game is over at the stadium,
Every soul waits to hear.
The sound of choir bells ringing,
That falls on each ear.

Those Bells of the Baylor Nation,
Starts shouting out it's evening Ring.
Ringing out those old sweet melodies,
For everyone to sing.

Everyday, every hour, on the hour,
The sweet bells start to ring.
Ringing songs and the time of day,
With each and every ding.

From far, wide and near,
You can hear the fight song play.
From the lakes and cliffs on the river,
That old nation had a good day.

Never slow, late, or even early.
The bells are always on time.
Bringing cheers by ringing and ringing,
For the Nations hearts to find.

Ring, ring, the Bells of Baylor nation,
Ring, Ring with laughter and song.
Send joy and peace, while everyone is listening,
Ring, Ring, Mighty Nation ring on.

COACH

The room was like a fiery furnace,
As the team ended it's pregame prayer.
Coach enters the players circle,
There was silence in the air.

He had a look of determination.
The first word he said was "team."
We are playing for the championship,
Let's play hard to reach our dream.

There are basic fundamentals to remember,
In order to move forward in this game.
Things to do and things to complete,
To reach our goals and fame.

Keep your guard up at all times,
Don't ever let it down.
Don't be take advantage of,
Don't get caught looking around.

Avoid being caught in the trap.
Look out for that old sucker play.
Use your head and think about,
How to stay out of the trap's way.

Overcome those hard fouls,
That will be committed against you.
Just play your game hard and fair,
Let every free-throw be true.

Remember to "rebound", "rebound", "rebound."
Control both sides of the boards.
"Press on", "Press on", defensively,
Don't take breaks you can't afford.

Know your role on the team.
Do your best playing your position.
It's going to get rough out there at times,
Don't give in to the opposition.

Always remember your game plan,
Execute it all the way.
Keep that plan in your head,
It will help your every play.

You only get out of this game,
The work you put into it each day.
Leave all you got on the court,
"You'll win" no matter what the score may say.

Sports were invented to create competition,
The more competition, the more fun.
The joy of the game is competing,
We compete in everything under the sun.

Make every play the big play,
It will make victory yours to behold.
In the end we'll be lifted as Champions,
That's our ultimate goal.

When coach finished, he stepped from the circle.
Every ear rested on his every word.
Then up went this thunderous yell,
The team ran out like a run-away herd.

Coach turned looked at his assistants,
He said our work here is done.
Let's go out and win this game,
But remember, the game was made to have fun.

Peace

When you play the game, give it your best,
Because God loves winners.
It matters not how good you are,
You can be a pro or a beginner.

It is also true that God do love,
Ones who are losers and sinners.
He loves all failures that exist on earth,
But above all, he loves those who are winners.

God loves the believers, he loves the achievers,
He loves those who have talents and use them.
We have muscles, and we have a brain,
We have the ability to win and please him.

If we know it or not, you may have forgot,
God has programmed us to be successful.
If we believe in ourselves and achieve our goals,
He will guide us and be helpful.

Through out the Bible there is one word,
Call it the basic word of the Good book.
That one word is triumph!
It can never be overlooked.

God has put his spirit in you,
His faith, his love and his blessings.
He expects for you to be great,
Through winning and following his lessons.

Dainian

Excuse me a minute to tip my hat,
To a man called LT.
He was a great football running back,
One of the best you would ever see.

He was Mr. Inside, Mr. Outside,
He could fly over the top.
He was the complete package, carrying the load,
he just couldn't be stopped.

He grew up in a central Texas town,
One of his (3x) great grandfathers was a slave.
His family carried their slave owner's name,
They will carry it to their graves.

A proud young man with character.
Proud to be a slave's great grandson.
A role model with a heart of Gold,
They named him LaDainian Tomlinson.

He didn't get a chance to carry the football,
Until his senior year in high school.
When he was finally given the chance,
He showed all of his God given tools.

He set all kinds of records that year,
He was given the award of All State.
He received a scholarship to play college ball
Where his records stand to this date.

Drafted number "5" overall in the pros,
His greatness continued on.
He was MVP, he was All Pro,
He was magic, he couldn't do no wrong.

He played on and ended his career.
He went into the Hall of Fame.
He never forgot where he came from,
He was proud of his Tomlinson name.

At his induction he gave a speech,
Like no other player had before.
He talked of God and Unity
That touched everyone. He got a standing "O."

A man so thankful for his blessings,
God gave him the gift of love.
Someone who never thinks of himself,
He is a gift to us from above.

I do not know if there will ever be
Another player like LT.
So upright and righteous in life
Sharing and happy as can be.

I would like to give him a toast
With a shot of that old #7.
With his gold jacket, he will get some gold wings
To fly around in Heaven.

Golden Boys

There's going to be a Reunion.
People are coming from far away.
The Golden Boys are coming home,
And this time they are going to stay.

They are the last of the big time spenders,
All drinks will be on the House.
Champagne, caviar and lobster,
They are high rollers with out a doubt.

All the old schoolers will be there.
Everyone you remember you'll see.
It'll be a day for celebration,
The prices of tickets are free.

Golf is their favorite activity.
They all have played at Pebble Beach.
Make sure you bring your gown and tux,
A class act is what they teach.

Make sure you get your tickets.
Be ready for good times and play.
The Golden Boys are coming home,
And this time they are going to stay.

Say No

Has anyone seen Little Slamming Sammy?
The last place he was spotted, he was in Miami.
He was going home to the Dominican Republic.
Since he left, his where abouts has not been public.

Where O Where is Big Mark Mac?
Hitting home runs with his oversize bat.
He and Sammy had a great home run race.
They left everyone behind at a hell of a pace.

Someone please tell me where is Rocket Clemens?
With his powerful fastball that made batters trimmer.
With the arm he had he was bound for the Hall of Fame.
Something went wrong, his calling never came.

Move over Roy Hobbs, make room for Barry Bonds,
Everything he hits turn into home runs.
Never seen anything like it, not even to this day.
He has knocked hundreds of balls into the San Francisco Bay.

Why, oh, why did they leave the public view?
Some said they played dirty, was unfaithful and untrue.
They turned to drugs to get fortune and fame,
And they sold their souls, to improve their game.

Oh what a pity the mistakes these men made,
They may be forgiven but their guilt will never fade.
They failed the hearts of many, for the greed they sought,
Their failure to reach greatness, is their own fault.

Brady

They called him the GOAT, Greatest of All Time.
Another one like him would be hard to find.
Around Boston they called him Tom Terrific,
He won football games from the Atlantic to the Pacific.

He had 6 rings from winning Super Bowls,
More Championship trophy's than anyone holds.
He could throw a pass through a needle's eye,
It was beauty in motion watching his passes fly.

He was built like a Nerd, no muscles at all.
Tall and lanky, he always answered the call.
Feared by many, cause he would pick you apart,
Loved by millions for his championship heart.

If you could catch passes, he would make you great.
All his passes come on time, so don't be late.
His 2 minute drills were just a thing of beauty.
The game to him came easy, cause it was his duty.

The Greatest of all Times is what many would say,
You will never see another, in all your dying days.
Tom Terrific Brady stands along at the top,
A quarterback above all, his legend will never stop.

Prime Time

It was the atmosphere of expectation,
Something big had to happen tonight.
Our team was losing the game.
But we were not quitting without a fight.

The fans and the team were expecting,
For something to save us from defeat.
It was gut check time for our team now,
They were determined not to get beat.

The clock stopped at two minutes,
Our team was behind by 4 points.
The outlook was dim, being the 4th quarter,
Our quarterback dislocated his shoulder joint.

It was third and five for the visitors,
The fans yelled out "Hold That Line".
To our surprise, our team sacked the quarterback.
Then a chant went out saying, "Prime Time".

"Prime Time", "Prime Time", "Prime Time".
The crowd's voices filled the air,
"Prime Time", "Prime Time", "Prime Time".
The announcer rose from his chair.

This atmosphere of expectation,
Was growing in everyone's head.
Everyone focused on number 1,
We knew our chances of winning were not dead.

Number 1 was known as "Prime Time",
"Prime Time" was his name.
He ran onto the field amidst all the cheers,
He is the most colorful in the game.

He stood on the field pacing slowly,
Checking how the wind would blow.
The fans in the stands was a buzzing,
It was time for the "Prime Time Show".

The visitors kicked a deep high sparrow,
It landed around the goal-line.
He fielded the ball and made two high steps,
Then he made a cut, right on a dime.

He started running down the sideline,
Other players seemed to be standing still.
The crowd kept on chanting "Prime Time",
As he went flying down the field.

Thirty yards from the goal line he started high stepping,
When he crossed the goal, he did the Boo-ga-lo.
The crowd went crazy with celebration,
"Prime Time", "Prime Time" had come through.

When he retires, they will hang his jersey from the rafters.
His golden shoes will go in the hall of fame.
He will have a section with glitter and lights,
Because "Prime Time", "Prime Time", is his name.

Jefferson Street Joe

I will tell you this story, of Jefferson Street Joe,
A college quarterback, who phased out as a pro.
He had a golden arm, and "Man," the kid could throw,
He was named after a street, he was named Jefferson Street Joe.

He wore white shoes, which was taped up to his knees,
He moved in the pocket, with the easiest of ease.
He could throw the touch pass, as soft as the summer breeze,
He could throw a bullet that would make cornerbacks freeze.

He was as quick as a cat, he had many fakes,
He was stylish and elegant, like a swan on the lake.
When the lights hit his shoes, he had moves like a snake,
He was the "Man" on the field, no prisoners did he take.

Joe was a character, he was lively and cool,
He was the man on campus, all his years in school.
But Joe developed a habit, it made him act a fool,
He started losing his talent, and his God given tools.

He lost everything as a pro, his habit stood in the way,
He hung out with the losers, and he forgot how to play,
Everyone prayed, that he would come back one day,
I will get it together, that is all Joe would say.

He went in and out of rehab, but his habit kept him down,
He never regained his glory, he wasn't the Man About Town.
In drugs and liquor, his problems he tried to drown,
In the end, it was sad, he was sometimes a clown.

O what could have been of Jefferson Street Joe?
He fell from the top, to as low as you can go.
His arm was golden, (like "Sinatra"), but man the Kid could Throw,
He was named after a street, he was Jefferson Street Joe.

Jefferson Street Joe

Thoughts of Oakland

The fog is thick,
There's coldness in the air.
Across the bay sit "The City",
Through the fog, it appears not there.

The exciting sounds of the night,
Sounds of horns, as vessels sail away.
The tooting sound of the Bart Train,
Delivering passengers ending the day.

The night lights of orange,
Creeps out the hillsides to play.
Traveling up narrow hilly streets,
Which gives a scenic view of the bay.

The Bay Bridge stands tall and majestic,
It's wounds from the Great Quake, has now healed.
Its lights disappear in the fog toward the city,
The traffic is constantly moving at will.

In the park as dawn is breaking,
Sit and watch a Tai-Chi display.
Everyone moves together in slow motion,
The ritual is how to start your day.

The gulls are gathering, primed for feeding,
They descend on food like birds of prey.
Everything that's edible will be eaten,
In the back alleys homeless people lay.

A child is awaken from his cardboard covers,
His parents are homeless, but not by choice.
They travel from homeless shelter after shelter,
Wondering if someone hears their voice.

As time passes, business opens.
Buy a cappuccino and discuss all the worldly faults.
Me, I enjoy walking Oakland's sandy beaches,
Feeding the gulls and reminiscing in my thoughts.

I Am Third

I am Third, I'm proud to say,
God and Others come before me.
I live each day with satisfaction,
Knowing that I am number three.

In this world of life's daily struggle,
Everyone strives to be the top two.
Number three is the number given me,
Being third my blessings are never few.

Do not be confused by these numbers,
Somewhere I am sure you have heard.
Put God first, others second,
And Me -- I am third.

Juice

It was around Juneteenth, the weather was hot,
I will never forget that day.
It was the day, they chased O.J.,
Down a L. A. Freeway.

There were police cars, following him afar, trying to take him away.
That sad day they chased O.J.,
Down a L.A. Freeway.

There were warrants on O.J, issued by the D.A., For the murders of Ron and Nicole.
"Oh" what a day, as they chased O.J.,
Down a L.A. Freeway.

A man who gave all, to be the best,
His deeds were good to say.
But on this day they chased O.J.,
Down a L.A. Freeway.

He stood for good, a hero to many,
His smile would steal you away.
It was a black day, as they chased O.J.,
Down a L.A. Freeway.

In the Bowls he thrilled many souls.
His records still stand today.
Let everyone pray, please help *O.J.*
Down that L.A. Freeway.

On the freeway they stood, hoping his chances were
good. The crowd cheered him along the way.
It was a very strange day, as they chased
O.J., Down a L.A. Freeway.

When he made it home, all fear was
gone, He turned himself in late that day.
As they took him away, it was "The Juice" last
Hurray, Down a L.A. Freeway.